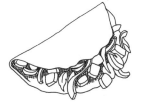

THE BEST 50
OMELETS

Coleen and Bob Simmons

BRISTOL PUBLISHING ENTERPRISES
San Leandro, California

Printed in the United States of America.

ISBN: 1-55867-256-7

Cover design: Frank J. Paredes
Cover photography: John A. Benson
Food stylist: Susan Devaty
Illustration: Hannah Suhr

ALL ABOUT OMELETS

The omelet's reputation for being difficult to make is more rumor than reality. Armed with a few basic techniques, even a beginner can turn out beautiful omelets in a short time. Once the art has been mastered, an infinite variety of omelets is possible.

Many ethnic cuisines have omelet-like dishes, but the thrifty, innovative French have elevated the omelet to its present perfection and popularity. It is no surprise that the world's favorite omelet is the classic French rolled omelet.

Omelets are delicious served plain, but it is the addition of fillings and sauces which make the endless variety of omelets possible. This book offers a large selection of omelets and fillings of all descriptions, but the most delicious ones may be those you create yourself! Have fun and use your imagination — that's what omelets are all about.

Once you have a basic knowledge of omelet-making, there are just four things needed for a perfect omelet: fresh eggs, butter or oil, the right pan and confidence. Confidence will come with practice.

Omelets are delicious served plain or embellished with fillings and sauces. The fillings offered here are a few of our favorites, but the possibilities are endless. Serve omelets often; they'll never be boring and with a little practice they can be made from start to finish in about three minutes.

Don't overlook omelets when entertaining. They are elegant, quickly made, satisfying and economical. An omelet accompanied by a tossed salad, croissants and a glass of wine is sure to please.

INGREDIENTS

Eggs should be as fresh as possible. They can be used right from the refrigerator or at room temperature. For a puffy omelet, you will find you get better volume if the whites are at room temperature. All recipes in this book were tested with U.S. Grade A large eggs, which weigh a little over 2 ounces each. If you use eggs of a different size, beat and measure, allowing 2 fluid ounces for each egg. Two fluid ounces of an egg substitute such as Second Nature or Eggbeaters is equivalent to 1 large egg.

Fresh, unsalted butter makes the best tasting omelets. Don't use too much; a teaspoon or two is enough to coat a nonstick pan. Vegetable oil with a few drops of dark sesame oil added works well in place of butter.

White or black pepper is traditionally used in omelets, but we like a few drops of red or green Tabasco Sauce instead. It blends easily throughout the eggs and improves the flavor. If an omelet tastes "hot" after cooking, reduce the amount of Tabasco Sauce a bit.

The addition of a teaspoon or two of water for each egg used slows the cooking of the eggs and tends to make the finished omelet lighter in texture.

PANS

Before the introduction of Teflon and other nonstick surfaces, carefully seasoned, mild steel pans were used to make omelets. Many cooks reserved a seasoned pan strictly for making omelets. If the pan was used for other foods, omelets were almost certain to stick until the pan was reseasoned.

The perfect omelet pan has a nonstick coating, fairly high sides to make rolling and folding the omelet easy, and is heavy enough to distribute the heat evenly, but light enough to heat quickly. Since some omelets are finished in the oven, the pan should have a metal or other heatproof handle.

PAN SIZE

Omelet pans vary in size. A pan that measures 7 to 8 inches across the top will produce a 5- to 6-inch omelet and is best for a 2-egg breakfast omelet. For European pans, which are measured in centimeters, this is size 22. Luncheon and supper omelets are usually made with 3 eggs in a pan that measures 9 to 10 inches, or 26 centimeters, across the top. A 4-egg omelet, just right for a lumberjack or a teenager, is made in a 12-inch or 30-centimeter pan. Rather than make French rolled omelets with more than 4 eggs, it is better to make a number of smaller ones.

The first section in this book begins with a basic French rolled omelet recipe with step-by-step directions to demonstrate that omelet-making is easy and uncomplicated. Don't be discouraged if your first try doesn't produce a pretty omelet. It will still taste good and the next one will turn out better. Once you master the art of making a perfect omelet, you'll find that nothing is easier, faster or more delicious.

BASIC FRENCH ROLLED OMELET AND FILLINGS

The French rolled omelet is discussed in detail to help omelet makers improve their technique. A well-made omelet is impressive and well worth the effort it takes to perfect this skill.

BASIC FRENCH ROLLED OMELET

This recipe is meant to serve as a beginner's guide and for reference. The formula makes it easy to vary the size of an omelet.

1-Egg Omelet	2-Egg Omelet	3-Egg Omelet
1 egg	2 eggs	3 eggs
1 tsp. water	2 tsp. water	1 tbs. water
1 dash salt	1 dash salt	1 dash salt
1 drop Tabasco Sauce	2 drops Tabasco Sauce	3 drops Tabasco Sauce
1 tsp. butter	2 tsp. butter	1 tbs. butter

Read the complete recipe and directions carefully, and gather all ingredients and equipment together before starting to cook.

Prepare filling as directed and set aside until needed.

Break eggs into a small bowl. Add water, salt and Tabasco Sauce. Beat with a table fork until whites and yolks are just blended, about 50 strokes or 20 seconds. The eggs should be combined but not foamy.

Place your omelet pan over moderately high heat. When pan is hot, add butter and rotate pan to coat evenly. When butter has stopped foaming but before it has browned, pour eggs into pan. Allow eggs to set for a few seconds before starting to stir them. Make circular movements around bottom of pan with the flat side of a table fork, lifting cooked egg up as you stir.

When omelet has set on the bottom, lift edge of omelet and tilt pan to allow any uncooked egg on top to flow under cooked portion. Shake pan vigorously to loosen omelet and prevent it from sticking. Smooth top of omelet with fork. Cook for a few seconds more. An omelet should be only slightly brown on the outside and still creamy, but not liquid, on the inside.

Spread about 2 tbs. filling along center of omelet. Fold omelet into thirds: fold edge opposite handle onto center, covering filling; then fold edge near handle over the middle.

Grasp handle of pan in your upturned palm. Roll omelet out onto a warm plate, seam-side down. Brush with a little melted butter for a nice sheen. Serve immediately.

Avoid having plate too hot, as omelet will continue to cook and toughen. The ideal plate is one that is very warm to the touch but can still be picked up with a bare hand.

As previously noted, we will refer to this basic omelet recipe throughout the book. Individual directions will be given for special recipes where needed.

FILLED OMELETS

A filled omelet is a simple variation of the classic French omelet. The technique is the same, but instead of a filling being rolled up in the omelet, the filling ingredients are sautéed with the butter in the omelet pan. Then the beaten eggs are poured over and everything becomes mixed as the omelet is stirred. It is rolled or folded and served in the same way as the French omelet.

BACON AND AVOCADO FILLING

Ripe avocado and crumbled bacon bits make a delicious omelet filling.

¹/₂ avocado
2 slices cooked bacon, crumbled
1 tbs. chopped fresh cilantro
¹/₂ tsp. chopped fresh chives
salt and pepper to taste

Mash avocado. Combine with bacon, cilantro, chives and a dash of salt and white pepper. Prepare omelets according to directions for *Basic French Rolled Omelet,* page 5. Fill with avocado and bacon mixture just before folding. Makes filling for 2 omelets.

BACON, SPINACH AND MUSHROOM FILLING

Serve this for a special brunch or cool weather lunch.

1 pkg. (10 oz.) frozen chopped
  spinach
6 slices bacon
8–10 fresh mushrooms,
  trimmed and sliced
5–6 green onions, white part
  only, thinly sliced

2 tbs. butter
2 tbs. flour
1 1/4 cups milk
1 tsp. Worcestershire sauce
salt and freshly ground pepper
  to taste

Defrost spinach, drain and squeeze as dry as possible. Set aside. Cut bacon into small pieces and fry until crisp. Remove bacon and sauté fresh mushrooms in bacon fat for 4 to 5 minutes. Stir in green onions and cook for another minute or two. Drain off excess bacon fat. Melt butter in a small saucepan. Add flour and cook for 2 minutes. Add milk, Worcestershire sauce, salt and pepper. Cook and stir until sauce thickens. Add spinach, mushrooms and bacon to sauce. Prepare omelets according to directions for *Basic French Rolled Omelet,* page 5. Before folding fill with sauce. Makes filling for 4 omelets.

CREAMED CHICKEN FILLING

Omelets filled with this rich chicken filling make a good luncheon dish for four. Serve with a mango salsa or a cranberry relish.

¼ cup butter or margarine
¼ cup flour
1½ cups milk
1 tsp. salt
½ tsp. white pepper
2 tbs. dry sherry

1 tsp. Dijon mustard
¼ cup diced roasted red bell
　pepper or pimiento
2 cups cubed cooked chicken
chopped fresh parsley for
　garnish

Melt butter in a small saucepan. Stir in flour and cook for 2 minutes. Gradually add milk and cook, stirring until sauce thickens. Stir in remaining ingredients and heat through. Prepare omelets according to directions for *Basic French Rolled Omelet,* page 5. Fill with creamed chicken mixture just before folding. Reserve a little of the filling for garnish and sprinkle with parsley. Makes filling for 4 omelets.

CHICKEN LIVER FILLING

This filling is for chicken liver lovers.

2 tbs. butter
1/3 cup chopped onion
1 cup sliced fresh mushrooms
1/2 lb. chicken livers
1/2 cup dry sherry
1/2 cup beef broth

1 tomato, peeled, seeded and
    chopped
2–3 tbs. sour cream
salt and white pepper to taste
chopped fresh chives for
    garnish

Melt butter in a medium skillet. Sauté onions and mushrooms over medium heat until soft. Add chicken livers to pan and sauté for 4 minutes. Remove onions, mushrooms and chicken livers and set aside. Turn heat to high. Pour in sherry and beef broth and reduce mixture by half. Return onions, mushrooms and chicken livers to pan with tomato and heat through. Remove from heat and stir in sour cream. Adjust seasoning. Prepare omelets according to directions for *Basic French Rolled Omelet,* page 5. Fill with chicken liver filling before folding. Reserve a little of the filling for garnish and sprinkle with chives. Makes filling for 3 to 4 omelets.

LOX AND ONION OMELET

Serve this deli classic with toasted bagels.

1 tbs. vegetable oil
1 medium-sized sweet onion, thinly sliced
3 oz. smoked salmon, thinly sliced
2 tbs. whipped cream cheese

Place a medium skillet over medium heat. Add oil and onion and cook until onions are soft and golden, about 8 minutes.

Prepare two 2-egg omelets according to directions for *Basic French Rolled Omelet,* page 5. Fill each with ½ of the onion and salmon. Top each with 1 tbs. cream cheese, fold and serve. Makes filling for 2 omelets.

SLOPPY JOE FILLING

This classic sandwich filling makes a great omelet.

¾ lb. lean ground beef
1 small onion, chopped
1 small clove garlic, minced
1 tbs. prepared chili powder
1 can (10½ oz.) beef stock
¼ tsp. dry mustard

1 tbs. Worcestershire sauce
3 tbs. tomato puree or catsup
few grains cayenne pepper, to
   taste
salt

In a medium skillet over medium-high heat, sauté beef until it browns. Crumble beef with a spatula as it cooks. Remove from pan and drain in a sieve. Pour off all but 2 tbs. pan drippings. Over low heat, sauté onion and garlic in remaining drippings for about 5 minutes until soft and transparent. Add chili powder and mix well. Return beef to pan. Stir in stock and remaining ingredients. Bring to a boil, lower heat and simmer uncovered for about 30 minutes, until most of moisture has evaporated. Season to taste, adding more cayenne or chili powder if desired. Prepare omelets according to directions for *Basic French Rolled Omelet,* page 5. Fill with meat mixture before folding. Makes filling for 4 omelets.

SAUSAGE AND PEPPERS FILLING

Sausage, peppers and onions give this omelet a savory Italian flavor.

4–6 small brown-and-serve sausages
1/2 large green bell pepper, diced
1/2 large red bell pepper, diced
1/2 medium onion, coarsely chopped
2 tbs. balsamic vinegar
1/4 cup dry white wine
salt and freshly ground pepper

Brown sausages in a medium skillet. Drain on paper towels. Cut into 1/2-inch pieces and set aside. Discard all but a little of the fat from skillet. Add peppers and onion. Sauté until soft but not brown, adding a little butter if necessary. Add sausages, vinegar and wine. Turn up heat and cook for 2 to 3 minutes until most of the liquid has evaporated. Prepare omelets according to directions for *Basic French Rolled Omelet,* page 5. Fill with peppers and sausages before folding. Makes filling for 2 omelets.

SALAMI AND ONION RING FILLING

Crisp onion rings give this omelet a nice crunchy texture.

4 eggs
4 drops Tabasco Sauce
salt
2 tbs. chopped fresh parsley
6 thin slices salami, diced
1/4 cup canned fried onion rings
Parmesan cheese for garnish

Beat eggs with Tabasco Sauce, salt, parsley and salami. Divide egg mixture to make 2 omelets. Prepare omelets according to directions for *Basic French Rolled Omelet,* page 5. Just before folding, sprinkle each with 1/2 of the onion rings. Sprinkle with a little Parmesan cheese for garnish. Makes 2 omelets.

ANCHOVY, CROUTON AND CHEESE FILLING

Crunchy croutons and cheese make an interesting omelet filling.

1 tbs. butter
1 tbs. cream cheese
2 anchovy fillets, washed, dried and finely chopped
$^{1}/_{2}$ tsp. brandy
2 slices bread
$^{1}/_{2}$ cup grated Parmesan cheese
parsley for garnish

Combine butter, cream cheese, anchovies and brandy. Mix to a smooth paste. Toast bread lightly in a toaster. Remove crusts. Spread with anchovy mixture. Sprinkle with Parmesan cheese. Place in a 350° oven for about 10 minutes until topping is lightly browned. Cut into $^{1}/_{2}$-inch croutons. Prepare omelets according to directions for *Basic French Rolled Omelet,* page 5. Before folding fill each with 2 tbs. croutons and 2 tbs. Parmesan or other mild cheese. Sprinkle with parsley. Makes filling for 4 omelets.

SARDINE AND CAPER FILLING

Sardines and capers make a satisfyingly salty combination that works well in this omelet.

1 can (4³/₈ oz.) skinless
  sardines packed in oil
1 tbs. butter
1 tbs. flour
³/₄ cup milk
1 tbs. Dijon mustard

1 tsp. Worcestershire sauce
¹/₈ tsp. white pepper
¹/₄ tsp. salt
nutmeg
1 tbs. capers, drained

Drain oil from sardines. Flake 3 sardines for sauce and leave remaining ingredients whole. Melt butter in a small saucepan. Add flour and cook for 2 minutes. Gradually stir in milk and remaining ingredients. Cook, stirring until sauce thickens. Stir in flaked sardines. Prepare 2 omelets according to directions for *Basic French Rolled Omelet*, page 5. Before folding, fill each omelet with 2 sardines. Fold over and spoon sauce over top. Makes filling and sauce for 2 omelets.

NEW ORLEANS FILLING

Here is a quick shrimp Creole omelet filling. Use small or medium-sized shrimp.

2 tbs. butter
1 cup finely chopped onion
1/2 cup finely chopped green
  bell pepper
1/3 cup finely sliced celery
1 small clove garlic, crushed
1/3 cup dry vermouth
2 medium tomatoes, peeled,
  seeded and chopped

1 tsp. Worcestershire sauce
4 drops Tabasco Sauce
1/2 tsp. dried thyme
1 dash cayenne pepper
1 bay leaf
2/3 lb. small peeled, deveined
  raw shrimp
salt and freshly ground pepper
  to taste

Melt butter in a large skillet. Sauté onion, green pepper, celery and garlic together. When almost soft, add vermouth. Add tomatoes and seasonings to pan. Cook over fairly high heat for about 10 minutes, stirring often. Add shrimp, salt and pepper. Lower heat and cook for about 2 minutes just until shrimp turns pink. Remove bay leaf. Prepare omelets according to directions for *Basic French Rolled Omelet*, page 5. Fill with shrimp mixture just before folding. Garnish the top of each omelet with a shrimp and a spoonful of sauce. Makes filling for 4 omelets.

CURRIED SHRIMP FILLING

Serve this with a little mango or pineapple chutney.

2 tbs. butter
2 tbs. flour
1/2 tsp. curry powder
1 1/4 cups milk

1/4 tsp. celery salt to taste
white pepper to taste
1/2 lb. small peeled, deveined,
    cooked shrimp

Melt butter in a small saucepan. Stir in flour and curry powder. Cook for 2 minutes. Gradually stir in milk and season with celery salt and pepper. Cook for 3 or 4 minutes, until sauce thickens. Stir in cooked shrimp and heat through. Prepare omelets according to directions for *Basic French Rolled Omelet,* page 5. Use part of the shrimp mixture for filling, reserving some for garnish. Makes filling for 2 to 3 omelets.

Variation: Substitute 1/2 lb. scallops for the shrimp. Cook for 2 to 3 minutes over low heat in 2 tbs. butter until scallops are just lightly browned.

CREAMED TUNA FILLING

Try this filling in French rolled omelets or in Baked Omelet Roll, *page 44.*

3 tbs. butter
3 tbs. flour
1 1/2 cups milk
1/2 tsp. celery salt
white pepper
1 can (6 1/2 oz.) tuna, drained
2 tbs. capers, drained
1/2 cup sliced green olives

Melt butter in a small saucepan. Add flour and cook for 2 minutes. Gradually add milk. Cook for 3 to 4 minutes, stirring over low heat until sauce thickens. Stir in celery salt, white pepper, tuna, capers and olives. Heat through. Prepare omelets according to directions for *Basic French Rolled Omelet,* page 5. Makes filling for 3 to 4 omelets.

CREAMED CAULIFLOWER
AND CHEESE FILLING

Feta cheese and black olives add Greek flavors to this filling.

1 tbs. butter
1 tbs. flour
1 cup milk
2–3 drops Tabasco Sauce
1/2 tsp. dried oregano
1/2 cup crumbled feta or goat
  cheese

1 1/2 cups coarsely chopped
  cooked cauliflower
8–10 kalamata black olives,
  pitted and coarsely chopped
salt and freshly ground black
  pepper
chopped fresh parsley

Melt butter in a small saucepan. Add flour and cook for 2 minutes. Gradually stir in milk and add Tabasco Sauce and oregano. Cook for 3 to 4 minutes, stirring until sauce thickens. Stir in cheese, cauliflower and olives. Season to taste. Cook for 1 to 2 minutes until filling is heated. Prepare omelets according to directions for *Basic French Rolled Omelet,* page 5. Before folding, fill with sauce and reserve a little of the mixture for topping. Sprinkle with garnish of parsley. Makes filling for 3 omelets.

SHERRY MUSHROOM FILLING

Sherry flavored mushrooms with sour cream make an excellent omelet filling.

2–3 tbs. butter
8–10 fresh mushrooms,
   trimmed and sliced
1 bunch green onions, sliced
$1/_4$ cup dry sherry or vermouth
$1/_2$ tsp. dried tarragon

$1/_2$ cup sour cream
1 dash nutmeg
salt and freshly ground black
   pepper to taste
chopped fresh parsley for
   garnish

In a medium skillet, sauté mushrooms and onions in butter for about 5 to 7 minutes, until soft. Add sherry and sauté until most of the liquid has evaporated. Stir in tarragon, sour cream, nutmeg, salt and pepper. Heat through but do not boil. Prepare omelets according to directions for *Basic French Rolled Omelet,* page 5. Fill with mushroom mixture just before folding. Sprinkle with parsley. Makes filling for 2 to 3 omelets.

THREE MUSHROOM FILLING

Use a combination of your favorite mushrooms for this filling.

³/₄ lb. mixed fresh mushrooms
2 tbs. vegetable oil
5 thinly sliced green onions,
   white part only
³/₄ oz. piece fresh ginger,
   peeled and finely minced
2 tbs. dry sherry
1 tsp. lemon juice

1 can (10½ oz.) beef broth
1 tsp. Worcestershire sauce
2 tsp. soy sauce
1 tbs. cornstarch
2 tbs. cold water
⅛ tsp. white pepper
chopped fresh cilantro for
   garnish

Clean, trim and cut mushrooms into ¼-inch slices. In a large nonstick skillet, heat oil and sauté fresh mushrooms, green onions and ginger in oil over high heat for 3 to 4 minutes. Add sherry, lemon juice, broth and soy sauce to skillet. Cook over medium-high heat for 8 to 10 minutes to reduce sauce by about ¼. Dissolve cornstarch in cold water. Over low heat, slowly add cornstarch to sauce, stirring constantly, until it becomes the consistency of heavy cream. It may not be necessary to add all of the cornstarch. Season with pepper. Sprinkle with cilantro. Makes filling for 4 omelets.

OMELET OLÉ

Here is a filling with a Spanish flavor.

2 tbs. olive oil
1/2 cup chopped onion
1/2 cup chopped green bell pepper
1 medium tomato, peeled, seeded and chopped
2 tbs. diced pimiento or roasted red bell pepper
1/2 tsp. paprika
2 tbs. diced ham
salt and freshly ground black pepper
chopped cilantro or parsley for garnish

Heat olive oil in a medium skillet. Sauté onion and green pepper for 7 or 8 minutes until soft. Add remaining ingredients and cook until mixture is fairly dry. Prepare omelets according to directions for *Basic French Rolled Omelet,* page 5. Fill omelet before folding. Makes filling for 2 omelets.

TOMATO, MUSHROOM, AND BACON FILLING

Make this when tomatoes are at the peak of their season.

2 tbs. butter, divided
1 large ripe tomato, peeled, seeded and chopped
4 large mushrooms, trimmed and sliced
1 tbs. chopped shallot, or 2 green onions, white part only, thinly
sliced
2 slices cooked bacon, crumbled
salt and freshly ground pepper
chopped fresh parsley or chives for garnish

Melt 1 tbs. butter in a small saucepan and cook tomato until soft and fairly dry. In a small skillet, sauté mushrooms and shallots in remaining tbs. butter for 3 to 4 minutes. Add mushrooms to tomatoes with crumbled bacon, salt and pepper. Simmer for 3 to 4 minutes to blend flavors. Makes filling for 2 omelets.

ZUCCHINI AND TOMATO FILLING

Use your garden fresh vegetables for this filling.

2 small zucchini (about 2 cups)
2 tomatoes, peeled, seeded
  and chopped
1 cup finely chopped onion
2 tbs. full-flavored olive oil
1 tsp. salt

1 tsp. Italian herb seasoning
1 pinch hot red pepper flakes
generous amount freshly
  ground black pepper
grated Parmesan cheese

Cut zucchini in half lengthwise and slice thinly. In a medium skillet, sauté onion in olive oil for 7 or 8 minutes until soft and translucent. Add sliced zucchini. Stir until zucchini is well coated with oil. Add tomatoes, salt, Italian herb seasoning, red pepper flakes and pepper. Sauté over medium heat until zucchini is tender and tomato juices have been absorbed. Mixture should be quite dry. Prepare omelets according to directions for *Basic French Rolled Omelet,* page 5. Just before folding, fill with zucchini mixture. Sprinkle with Parmesan cheese. Makes filling for 4 omelets.

ASPARAGUS AND LEMON CRUMB OMELET

Make this omelet for luncheon when fresh asparagus is in season.

3 large eggs
3 drops Tabasco Sauce
1 tbs. water
1 dash salt
2 tbs. unsalted butter

2 tbs. grated fresh breadcrumbs
3/4 cup diced cooked
   asparagus, in 3/4-inch dice
grated zest of 1/2 lemon
chopped fresh parsley or chives

Beat eggs, Tabasco Sauce, water and salt with a fork in a small bowl until well combined. Set aside. Melt butter in a 10-inch non-stick skillet or well-seasoned omelet pan. When butter foams, add breadcrumbs and cook over low heat until they start to color. Add asparagus and lemon zest. Continue to cook until crumbs are golden brown. Crumbs will brown very quickly once they start coloring. Pour egg mixture on top of asparagus mixture. Make circular movements around bottom of pan with the flat side of a table fork to incorporate filling and allow uncooked egg to flow under and set. Fold omelet and turn out onto a warm plate. Garnish with chopped parsley or chives. Serves 2.

BROCCOLI AND PROSCIUTTO OMELET

Use leftover cooked broccoli for a quick omelet.

3 large eggs
3 drops Tabasco Sauce
1 tbs. water
1 dash salt
1 tbs. butter
1/3 cup chopped cooked
   broccoli

1 tbs. diced prosciutto or
   country ham
2 green onions, white part only,
   thinly sliced
chopped fresh parsley for
   garnish

Beat eggs, Tabasco Sauce, water and salt with a fork in a small bowl until well combined. Set aside. Melt butter in a 10-inch non-stick skillet or well-seasoned omelet pan. When foaming, add broccoli, prosciutto and green onions. Cook over low heat for 2 to 3 minutes. Pour egg mixture into skillet on top of broccoli. Make circular movements around bottom of pan with the flat side of a table fork to incorporate filling and allow uncooked egg to flow under and set. Fold omelet and turn out onto a warm plate. Garnish with chopped parsley.

CRAB AND AVOCADO OMELET

A good choice for a special luncheon. Accompany with a green salad and a glass of white wine.

3 large eggs
3 drops Tabasco Sauce
1 tbs. water
1 dash salt
1 tbs. butter
½ cup flaked crabmeat

2 green onions, white part only,
   thinly sliced
½ cup diced avocado
3–4 basil leaves, cut into thin
   ribbons, for garnish

Beat eggs, Tabasco Sauce, water and salt with a fork in a small bowl until well combined. Set aside. Melt butter in a 10-inch non-stick skillet or well-seasoned omelet pan. When foaming, add crab and green onions. Cook for 2 to 3 minutes until butter is lightly browned. Pour egg mixture into skillet on top of crab and onion mixture. Add diced avocado. Make circular movements around bottom of pan with the flat side of a table fork to incorporate filling and allow uncooked egg to flow under and set. Fold omelet and turn out onto a warm plate. Garnish with basil ribbons.

SHRIMP AND WALNUT OMELET

Walnuts add both flavor and texture to this omelet.

3 large eggs
3 drops Tabasco Sauce
1 tbs. water
1 dash salt
1 tbs. butter
3–4 drops sesame oil
1/2 cup small cooked shrimp

1 green onion, white part only,
   thinly sliced
3 tbs. coarsely chopped
   toasted walnuts
chopped fresh cilantro leaves
   for garnish

Beat eggs, Tabasco Sauce, water and salt with a fork in a small bowl until well combined. Set aside. Heat butter and oil in a 10-inch nonstick skillet or well-seasoned omelet pan. When foaming, add shrimp, onion and walnuts. Cook for 2 to 3 minutes over low heat until butter is lightly browned. Pour egg mixture into skillet on top of shrimp. Make circular movements around bottom of pan with the flat side of a table fork to incorporate filling and allow uncooked egg to flow under and set. Fold omelet and turn out onto a warm plate. Garnish with cilantro leaves.

SAUTÉED SCALLOPS OMELET

Small bay scallops, parsley and garlic are cooked with the eggs in this omelet.

3 large eggs
3 drops Tabasco Sauce
1 tbs. water
1 dash salt
flour seasoned with a little salt
    and white pepper, for coating

1 tbs. butter
1/2 cup bay scallops
1/4 tsp. minced garlic
1 tsp. grated lemon zest
1 tsp. minced fresh parsley

Beat eggs, Tabasco Sauce, water and salt with a fork in a small bowl until well combined. Set aside. Lightly flour scallops and shake off excess. Melt butter in a 10-inch nonstick skillet or well-seasoned omelet pan. Add scallops and garlic to foaming butter. Cook for 2 to 3 minutes over low heat until scallops are just lightly browned. Pour egg mixture into skillet on top of scallops. Add parsley. Make circular movements around bottom of pan with the flat side of a table fork to incorporate filling and allow uncooked egg to flow under and set. Fold omelet and turn out onto a warm plate.

GREEN BEAN OMELET

Green beans and bacon are a classic combination.

3 large eggs
3 drops Tabasco Sauce
1 tbs. water
1 dash salt
1 tbs. butter
1/2 cup pieces cooked green beans, 3/4-inch
2 tbs. cooked crumbled bacon

2 green onions, white part only, thinly sliced
1 pinch dried thyme
freshly ground black pepper to taste
chopped fresh parsley or chives for garnish

Beat eggs, Tabasco Sauce, water and salt with a fork in a small bowl until well combined. Set aside. Melt butter in a 10-inch non-stick skillet or well-seasoned omelet pan. When foaming add green beans, bacon, green onions, thyme and black pepper. Cook over low heat until butter is lightly browned. Pour egg mixture into skillet on top of green beans. Make circular movements around bottom of pan with the flat side of a table fork to incorporate filling and allow uncooked egg to flow under and set. Fold omelet and turn out onto a warm plate. Garnish with parsley or chives.

MUSHROOM OMELET

Mushrooms make terrific omelets.

3 large eggs
3 drops Tabasco Sauce
1 tbs. water
1 pinch dried mustard powder
1 dash salt
1 tbs. butter
4 fresh mushrooms, trimmed and sliced

2 green onions, white part only, thinly sliced
1 tsp. chopped fresh tarragon leaves, or 1/4 tsp. dried
chopped fresh parsley for garnish

Beat eggs, Tabasco Sauce, water, mustard powder and salt with a fork in a small bowl until well combined. Set aside. Melt butter in a 10-inch nonstick skillet or well-seasoned omelet pan. When foaming, add mushrooms and green onions. Cook over medium heat for 4 to 5 minutes. Pour egg mixture into skillet on top of mushrooms. Make circular movements around bottom of pan with the flat side of a table fork to incorporate filling and allow uncooked egg to flow under and set. Fold omelet and turn out onto a warm plate.

MORE OMELETS PLAIN AND FANCY

This section could be called a potpourri of omelet recipes. Some are for old favorites, such as puffy omelets, while some of the others offer unusual ideas for serving plain omelets.

Puffy omelets with their soufflé-like consistency are as pretty as they are delicious. Usually served with a filling and a sauce, they make marvelous luncheon and late-supper entrées. Their lovely texture is achieved by separating the eggs and folding the stiffly beaten whites into the yolks, which have been combined with the seasonings and other ingredients. Puffy omelets are started on the stovetop and then finished in a hot oven. One omelet usually makes two or more servings.

PUFFY OMELET

This is the basic recipe for a puffy omelet. You can serve it plain or with your choice of filling.

4 large eggs, separated
4 drops Tabasco Sauce
1 dash salt
2 tbs. cold water
1 tbs. unsalted butter

Preheat broiler, positioning a rack about 6 inches from heat source. In a mixer bowl, add salt and Tabasco Sauce to egg whites. Beat until stiff peaks form. In a small bowl, beat egg yolks and water until foamy. Fold into egg whites. Heat butter in a 10-inch nonstick skillet with an ovenproof handle. When butter foams, add egg mixture to pan and allow to set on the bottom for a few seconds. Finish cooking by placing under broiler until top is lightly browned. Remove from oven. If using filling, spoon most of the filling over ½ of the omelet, fold remaining ½ over and and top with remaining filling. Serve immediately on warm plates. Serves 2.

THIN OMELET

Use thin omelets to make a Bacon and Tomato Breakfast Sandwich, *page 40, or use them to make a layered omelet with* Pesto Omelet Filling, *page 42.*

5 large eggs   salt
3 tbs. cream   4 tsp. unsalted butter
4 drops Tabasco Sauce

In a medium bowl, beat eggs with cream, Tabasco Sauce and salt and pour into a measuring cup. Use ¼ of the mixture for each omelet. Melt 1 tsp. butter in an 8-inch nonstick skillet or well-seasoned omelet pan. When butter is foaming, pour in ¼ of the egg mixture. Stir center with fork and lift eggs around edges so uncooked part can flow under cooked eggs. When set, turn out onto a plate and add another 1 tsp. butter to pan. When foamy, add another ¼ of the mixture. Continue until you have cooked 4 omelets.

Note: This recipe will also make 5 thinner omelets if you divide egg mixture into 5 parts.

PROVENÇAL OMELET SANDWICH

This omelet filling can also be incorporated into a frittata or used to fill individual omelets.

2 tbs. olive oil
6–8 fresh mushrooms, trimmed and sliced
1 large onion, chopped
1/2 red or green bell pepper, chopped
2 zucchini, thinly sliced
4 Japanese eggplants, trimmed and diced (about 1 lb.)
3 tomatoes, peeled, seeded and chopped
1 clove garlic, minced
2 tsp. fresh thyme leaves
salt and freshly ground pepper to taste
3 tbs. grated Parmesan cheese
2–3 tbs. grated Swiss or Gruyère cheese
2 *Puffy Omelets,* page 36

Heat oven to 375.° Heat olive oil in a large skillet. Sauté sliced mushrooms over high heat for 2 to 3 minutes. Remove mushrooms from pan and set aside. Add onion to skillet and sauté for 5 to 6 minutes over low heat, until almost soft. Add red pepper, zucchini and eggplant. Cook for 5 minutes. Add tomatoes and seasonings to vegetables. Cover and cook over low heat for 10 to 15 minutes. Add mushrooms and cook uncovered for 10 minutes or until mixture is fairly dry. Stir in Parmesan cheese.

Cook 2 *Puffy Omelets* in a 10-inch omelet pan according to instructions. Place an omelet on an ovenproof serving platter. Spread with Provençal filling. Top with second omelet. Sprinkle with grated cheese. Place in oven until cheese melts. Cut into wedges to serve. Makes 3 to 4 servings.

BACON AND TOMATO
BREAKFAST SANDWICH

Strips of bacon and sliced tomatoes are layered between thin egg omelets and topped with Avocado Sauce.

AVOCADO SAUCE
2 tbs. unsalted butter
2 tbs. flour
1 1/4 cups milk
1/4 tsp. salt
1/4 tsp. dry mustard
white pepper
1 ripe avocado, peeled and diced

4 *Thin Omelets,* page 37
6 slices cooked bacon
3 thin slices tomato

Melt butter in a small saucepan. Stir in flour. Cook for 2 minutes. Gradually add milk. Season with salt, dry mustard and pepper. Cook for 3 to 4 minutes, stirring until sauce thickens. Remove from heat and add diced avocado.

Make 4 *Thin Omelets*. Leave flat.

Heat oven to 350.° Place an omelet on an ovenproof serving plate. Spread with a little of the *Avocado Sauce.* Break 3 bacon slices into large pieces. Place on top of sauce. Top with another thin omelet. Spread with *Avocado Sauce* and top with tomato slices. Top with next omelet. Again spread with *Avocado Sauce* and remaining bacon. Top with last omelet. Pour remaining *Avocado Sauce* over last omelet. Place in oven for 10 minutes to heat through. Makes 2 servings.

PESTO FILLING
FOR A LAYERED THIN OMELET

Pesto filling alternates with tomatoes and ham between Thin Omelet *layers, and is then cut into pie-shaped wedges.*

2 tbs. olive oil
1 tbs. lemon juice
1/4 cup chopped fresh Italian flat parsley leaves
1 cup fresh basil leaves
1 small clove garlic, mashed
1/2 tsp. salt
1/2 tsp. sugar
1/4 cup pine nuts or slivered almonds, lightly toasted
1/4 cup grated Parmesan cheese
1 cup peeled, seeded, chopped tomatoes
1 cup slivered ham pieces or cooked, crumbled bacon pieces
additional grated Parmesan cheese for topping
5 *Thin Omelets*, page 37

Place olive oil, lemon juice, parsley, basil, garlic, salt, sugar and nuts in a blender container or food processor workbowl. Puree until fairly smooth. Stir in cheese. Prepare 5 *Thin Omelets* according to directions. Leave flat.

Heat oven to 350.° Place a cooked omelet on an ovenproof serving plate. Spread omelet with ½ of the pesto filling. Place another cooked omelet directly on top of the first. Distribute chopped tomatoes over it. Top with another omelet. Cover this with ham or bacon. The next omelet should be spread with remaining pesto filling. Top with last omelet. Sprinkle with a little more Parmesan cheese. Place in oven for 12 to 15 minutes to heat through. Cut into wedges to serve. Makes 4 to 5 servings.

Variation: Prepare omelets according to directions for *Basic French Rolled Omelet,* page 5. Fill with *Pesto Filling* just before folding.

BAKED OMELET ROLL

Fill with Creamed Tuna Filling, *page 21, or* Provençal Omelet Sandwich *filling, page 38.*

2 tbs. unsalted butter
2 tbs. flour
1 cup milk
$\frac{1}{2}$ tsp. salt
white pepper to taste
4 large eggs, separated
4 drops Tabasco Sauce

Heat oven to 350.° Melt butter in a small saucepan. Stir in flour. Cook for 2 minutes. Gradually add milk. Cook over low heat for 3 to 4 minutes, until sauce thickens. Add salt and pepper. In a small bowl, beat egg yolks with Tabasco Sauce. Carefully combine egg yolk mixture with a little of the hot mixture and gradually add eggs to sauce. Remove from heat.

In a mixer bowl, beat egg whites until stiff. Fold into slightly cooled sauce. Butter a 15-x-10-x-1-inch jelly roll pan and line with parchment or waxed paper. Butter and lightly flour paper. Spread egg mixture evenly in pan and bake for 15 to 20 minutes, until puffy and lightly browned. Carefully turn out on a clean kitchen towel. Remove paper. Gently roll up omelet with towel, rolling from the long side. Place towel-covered omelet roll on a rack and cool for a few minutes.

Gently unroll and spread with hot filling, reserving a little of the filling for garnish. Reroll and cut into serving slices. Spoon some of the reserved filling over each serving. Makes 4 servings.

Variation: Add 1 cup minced chicken or ham, or $1/2$ cup grated cheese or 1 cup cooked, well drained, finely chopped spinach to egg mixture before folding in egg whites. Increase baking time about 5 minutes.

PIZZA OMELET

Put your favorite pizza topping on an omelet.

1 tbs. olive oil
3 tbs. finely minced onion
1 can (8 oz.) tomato sauce
1 tsp. dried oregano
salt and freshly ground pepper to taste
three *2-Egg Omelets,* page 5
3 tbs. butter
sliced cheese for topping
sliced salami or sausage for topping
sliced black olives for topping
sliced sautéed fresh mushrooms for topping

Preheat broiler. Heat olive oil in a small skillet. Sauté onion for 3 to 4 minutes. Add tomato sauce, oregano, salt and pepper. Simmer for 5 minutes to blend flavors and thicken sauce slightly.

Prepare eggs for three 2-egg omelets. Melt 1 tbs. butter in a nonstick 8-inch skillet with ovenproof handle. When butter coats pan, pour in one 2-egg omelet. Shake and stir over low heat until eggs are barely set. Spoon 1/3 of the tomato sauce over eggs. Top with 1/3 of the cheese, salami, olives and mushrooms. Place under broiler until cheese melts. Slide open-faced omelet onto heated serving plate.

Repeat for remaining 2 omelets. Makes 3 servings.

COUNTRY-STYLE OMELET

This hearty omelet is made with potatoes and served flat.

6 slices bacon
1 large baking potato, peeled
and cut into ¼-inch dice
5–6 green onions, white part
only, thinly sliced
1 tbs. unsalted butter
1–2 tomatoes, peeled, seeded
and chopped (about 1 cup)

2 tbs. chopped fresh parsley
6 large eggs
2 tsp. water
4 drops Tabasco Sauce
salt and pepper

Cut bacon into small pieces. Fry until crisp in a nonstick 9-inch skillet with ovenproof handle. Lift bacon from pan with a slotted spoon and set aside. Reserve bacon fat. Add potatoes to skillet and sauté slowly. When almost done, add green onions and cook until potatoes are lightly browned and onion is wilted. Pour off any remaining fat from skillet. Melt butter in a small saucepan. Add tomatoes and cook over fairly high heat for 3 to 4 minutes until most of the liquid has evaporated. Distribute potatoes and onion evenly around skillet. Sprinkle bacon pieces over potatoes. Add cooked tomatoes and chopped parsley.

Preheat broiler. Position oven rack about 6 inches from heat source. Beat 6 eggs with water, Tabasco Sauce, salt and pepper. Pour eggs over potato mixture. Cook over low heat until eggs start to set. Lift eggs around sides of the pan so uncooked portion flows underneath. Place under broiler and cook for 5 to 10 minutes, until top is set and starting to lightly brown. Remove from oven and carefully slide out of pan onto a serving plate. Cut into wedges to serve. Makes 4 servings.

VARIATIONS

• Omit bacon; fry potatoes in vegetable oil and use sliced salami, diced ham, thinly sliced Italian sausage, smoked salmon or sardines.

• Omit tomato and add ¾ cup grated Swiss cheese or Parmesan cheese.

• In addition to onion, add green pepper, green chiles, pimiento and fresh basil or cilantro.

EGG FOO YUNG

This is a Chinese-style omelet served with a brown sauce.

6 large eggs
1 1/2 cups fresh bean sprouts, broken into 1-inch pieces
1/3–1/2 cup diced ham, small shrimp or other cooked meat
1 cup thinly sliced fresh mushrooms
4–5 green onions, white part only, thinly sliced
1 tbs. dry sherry
salt and white pepper to taste
Chinese Foo Yung Sauce, follows

Heat oven to 150.° Combine all ingredients in a large bowl. Stir just until eggs are barely mixed. Heat a nonstick 8-inch skillet or well-seasoned omelet pan with vegetable oil to cover bottom of pan to a depth of 1/8 inch. Over medium heat, add 1/4 of the egg mixture and cook until set. Turn over to cook the other side. Lift from pan and place on paper towels to drain. Hold in warm oven until 3 remaining omelets have been cooked. Serve with *Chinese Foo Yung Sauce.* Makes 4 large omelets.

CHINESE FOO YUNG SAUCE

2 cups chicken or beef broth
1 tbs. soy sauce
1 tsp. grated fresh ginger
4 tsp. cornstarch
2 tbs. dry sherry

Bring broth, soy sauce and ginger to boil in a small saucepan. Dissolve cornstarch in sherry and stir into boiling broth. Simmer for 1 to 2 minutes until thickened. Makes 2 cups sauce.

BAKED ARTICHOKE OMELET

Frozen or canned artichoke hearts work well for this dish.

6 cooked artichoke hearts
2 tbs. olive oil
3 green onions, white part only, thinly sliced
4 large eggs
2 tbs. diced roasted red bell pepper or pimiento
2 tbs. chopped fresh basil
$1/4$ tsp. salt
2 tbs. unsalted butter
$1/3$ cup grated Parmesan cheese
chopped fresh parsley for garnish

Heat oven to 375.° Cut artichoke hearts into small pieces. Heat olive oil in a nonstick 8-inch skillet with an ovenproof handle. Sauté artichoke hearts and green onions for 2 to 3 minutes. Remove from pan. In a medium bowl, beat eggs, red pepper, basil and salt together. Melt butter in same skillet used for artichokes and pour in eggs. Spread artichoke mixture over eggs. Cook over low heat until eggs have set slightly. Sprinkle with cheese and place in oven for 8 to 10 minutes, until top of omelet has set and is lightly browned. Remove from oven and carefully slide onto a serving plate. Cut into wedges and serve warm. Garnish with parsley. Makes 2 to 3 servings.

JOE'S SPECIAL

This San Francisco classic isn't really an omelet, but it is so good that it is included here. For brunch, serve with a salad and lightly toasted sourdough bread.

½ lb. ground chuck
½ lb. mushrooms, trimmed and coarsely chopped
1 medium onion, chopped, about 1 cup
2 cloves garlic, finely chopped
1 pkg. (10 oz.) frozen chopped spinach, defrosted and squeezed
very dry
6 large eggs
salt and freshly ground black pepper to taste

Place a 12-inch nonstick skillet over medium heat. Crumble ground meat into skillet and fry until meat is lightly browned, breaking it up into small pieces with a spatula. Pour off all but 1 tbs. of the rendered fat. Add mushrooms, onions and garlic and cook for 4 to 5 minutes until onion is soft and mushroom liquid is released. Add spinach and continue cooking until all liquid has evaporated.

Break eggs into a bowl, season with salt and pepper and whisk to combine. Pour eggs into skillet and stir with a fork to incorporate meat and vegetables. Continue scrambling until eggs are cooked through. Serve on warm plates. Pass the ketchup, if you like.

GOOD FOR YOU OMELET

There are several good egg substitute products on the market. They usually are mostly egg whites and will make a very good omelet.

3 oz. Second Nature,
   Eggbeaters or other egg
   substitute
1/4 tsp. salt

1 tsp. vegetable oil
3–4 drops sesame seed oil
grated Parmesan cheese for
   filling, optional

Combine Second Nature and salt. Beat with a fork until slightly foamy. Heat vegetable oil and sesame seed oil in a nonstick 8-inch skillet or well-seasoned omelet pan. Pour in Second Nature mixture. Prepare omelets according to directions for *Basic French Rolled Omelet,* page 5. Sprinkle with 2 tbs. cheese or other desired filling before folding.

GOOD FOR YOU HERB OMELET

Combine 1 tbs. chopped fresh parsley, 2 tbs. chopped fresh basil and 1 tsp. chopped chives with Second Nature or other egg substitute. Cook as directed.

FRITTATAS

When making a frittata, the Italian word for omelet, all ingredients including the eggs are mixed together and poured into a heated ovenproof skillet containing oil. When the eggs are partially set, the frittata is placed under the broiler to finish. Frittatas are good served warm or at room temperature and make excellent appetizers, lunch box snacks or picnic fare.

These recipes use 4 eggs to make a frittata in an 8-inch skillet. This yields a 6-inch frittata, enough for 2 large servings or 3 to 4 smaller ones. All of these recipes can be doubled successfully using a 10-inch skillet, which produces an 8-inch frittata.

For the diet-conscious, egg substitutes such as Second Nature or Eggbeaters make very good frittatas when used in place of whole eggs in these recipes. Use 1 cup (8 ounces) for a small frittata and 2 cups (16 ounces) for a large one.

ZUCCHINI FRITTATA

Use a food processor to make quick work of grating the zucchini.

2 cups grated zucchini
½ tsp. salt
2 tbs. full-flavored olive oil
2 tomatoes, peeled, seeded and chopped
4 large eggs, lightly beaten
5 green onions, white part only, thinly sliced
½ cup grated Parmesan cheese
1 tsp. dried basil
1 tsp. Dijon mustard
½ tsp. salt
freshly ground black pepper to taste
1 dash nutmeg

Grate zucchini coarsely. Place in a sieve, lightly sprinkle with salt and allow to stand for 15 to 20 minutes. Rinse zucchini under cold water and squeeze as dry as possible. Heat olive oil in a 7- or 8-inch skillet with ovenproof handle. In a large bowl, combine zucchini with remaining ingredients. Mix well and pour into heated pan. Cook over low heat until eggs begin to set. Lift eggs around the sides of pan so the uncooked portion flows under the cooked part. When partially set, place under a heated broiler about 6 inches away from heat source for 5 to 10 minutes or until top is set and starts to brown. Remove frittata from oven and carefully slide out of pan onto a plate lined with paper toweling. Let drain. Cut into wedges. Serve warm or at room temperature. Makes 2 to 3 servings.

GARBANZO BEAN FRITTATA

Serve with your favorite prepared salsa.

2 tbs. olive oil
1/2 cup finely chopped onion
1/4 cup chopped pimiento or roasted red bell pepper
1/4 cup sliced ripe olives
1 cup cooked garbanzo beans
2 tbs. chopped fresh parsley
1/2 tsp. dried basil
1/2 tsp. paprika
4 large eggs, lightly beaten
salt and pepper
1 tbs. olive oil
grated Parmesan cheese for topping

Heat olive oil in a 7- to 8-inch skillet with an ovenproof handle. Sauté onions for 7 or 8 minutes until soft. Place onions in a small bowl. Combine with pimiento, olives, garbanzo beans, parsley, basil, eggs, salt and pepper. Mix well. Add 1 tbs. olive oil to oil remaining in skillet. Pour in egg mixture. Cook over low heat until eggs start to set. Lift eggs around sides of pan so the uncooked portion flows under the cooked part. When partially set, top with Parmesan cheese. Place under a heated broiler about 6 inches away from the heat source for 5 to 10 minutes or until top is set and starts to brown. Remove from oven and carefully slide out of pan onto a plate lined with paper toweling. Let drain. Cut into wedges. Serve warm or at room temperature. Makes 2 to 3 servings.

SPINACH FRITTATA

The eggs are beaten separately to make a puffier frittata.

1 pkg. (10 oz.) frozen chopped spinach
4 large eggs, separated
1 dash nutmeg
5–6 green onions, white part only, thinly sliced
1 tbs. Dijon mustard
salt and freshly ground black pepper to taste
1 tbs. chopped fresh parsley
1 tbs. chopped fresh basil, or 1 1/2 tsp. dried
1/3 cup grated Parmesan cheese
3 tbs. olive oil
grated Parmesan cheese for topping

Defrost spinach, drain and squeeze as dry as possible. In a large bowl, combine spinach, egg yolks, seasonings, onions and Parmesan cheese. Mix well. In a separate bowl, beat egg whites until stiff peaks form. Gently fold into spinach mixture. Heat olive oil in a 7- to 8-inch skillet with ovenproof handle. Pour in egg mixture. Cook over low heat until eggs start to set. Lift eggs around sides of pan so the uncooked portion flows underneath. Sprinkle with Parmesan cheese. When partially set, place under a heated broiler about 6 inches from heat source for 5 to 10 minutes or until top is set and starts to brown. Remove from oven and carefully slide out of pan onto a plate lined with paper toweling. Drain and cut into wedges. Serve warm or at room temperature. Makes 2 to 3 servings.

GREEN CHILE RICE FRITTATA

Leftover rice is perfect for this dish. Dense and creamy, this satisfying breakfast frittata can be made with an egg substitute if desired. Prepared red or green chunky salsa makes an easy and complementary topping.

4 large eggs or 8 oz. egg substitute
$^1/_4$ cup minced green onion
$^1/_4$ tsp. green Tabasco Sauce
1 tbs. grated Parmesan cheese, plus more for sprinkling
$^1/_4$ tsp. salt
1$^3/_4$ cups cooked rice, cooled and divided
3 tbs. canned diced green chiles with 1 tbs. liquid
2 tsp. olive oil
prepared chunky mild or medium salsa to taste

Place an oven shelf about 6 inches from the heat source and preheat broiler.

Place eggs, onion, Tabasco Sauce, cheese, salt and 3/4 cup of the cooked rice in a blender container. Blend on high for 15 seconds or until smooth. Add green chiles with their liquid and 1 cup of the reserved rice to blender container. Pulse once or twice to combine.

Heat olive oil in a 7- to 8-inch nonstick skillet with ovenproof handle over medium heat. Add egg mixture and reduce heat to low. Cook over low heat until eggs begin to set. Lift eggs around the sides of pan so the uncooked portion flows underneath. When eggs have set around sides of pan, sprinkle about 2 tbs. more Parmesan over the top and place under broiler. When center of frittata has just set and is lightly browned, remove from oven. Cut into wedges and serve warm or at room temperature. Spoon mild or medium chunky salsa over wedges if desired. Makes 4 to 6 servings.

FRITTATAS

FRITTATA PROVENÇAL

The filling from the Provençal Omelet Sandwich *is used to make this frittata.*

1 1/2–2 cups *Provençal Omelet Sandwich* filling, page 38
4 large eggs, lightly beaten
salt and freshly ground pepper
1/2 cup grated cheddar or Monterey Jack cheese
2 tbs. olive oil

Combine *Provençal Omelet Sandwich* filling with eggs, salt, pepper and cheese. Mix well. Heat oil in a 7- to 8-inch skillet with ovenproof handle. Pour egg mixture into heated pan and cook over low heat until eggs start to set. Lift eggs around the sides of pan so uncooked portion flows under the cooked part. When partially set, place under a heated broiler about 6 inches away from the heat source for 5 to 10 minutes or until top is set and starts to lightly brown. Remove from oven and carefully slide out of pan onto a plate lined with paper toweling. Let drain. Cut into wedges. Serve warm or at room temperature. Makes 2 to 3 servings.

DESSERT OMELETS

If an easy, light dessert is what you want, omelets are the answer. Omelets can be simple or elaborate, but never heavy. Especially pretty are flaming omelets. Lower the lights, pour warmed rum or liqueur over prepared omelets and ignite. Your guests will love the effect.

Dessert omelets have sugar, cream and flavorings added to the eggs before cooking. The custard-like mixture is cooked in butter until the bottom sets slightly, and it is finished under a hot broiler. The filling can be as simple as jam or a fruit sauce spooned on the omelet before it is folded. Sifted confectioners' sugar dusted over the top adds a pretty finishing touch. Fluffy, soufflé-like dessert omelets make a glamorous appearance, too. They can be topped with a delicious sauce, garnished with nuts and cut into wedges. Serve on your prettiest dessert plate.

The dessert omelets in this chapter can all be made with either the *Basic Dessert Omelet,* page 68, or the *Puffy Viennese Dessert Omelet,* page 69.

BASIC DESSERT OMELET

This is perfect for almost any sweet filling.

2 large eggs
2 tsp. sugar
1 tbs. heavy cream
1 dash salt
1 pinch white pepper
1–2 drops (less than $\frac{1}{8}$ tsp.) almond or lemon extract
1 tbs. unsalted butter
confectioners' sugar for dusting

In a small bowl, combine all ingredients except butter and confectioners' sugar. Beat well with a fork. Heat butter in a nonstick 8-inch skillet with an ovenproof handle. When foaming, add omelet mixture. Allow bottom to set slightly. Finish under a hot broiler until top is set and lightly browned. Fill with jam or other dessert filling. Fold and dust with confectioners' sugar.

PUFFY VIENNESE DESSERT OMELET

Serve plain, fill with fresh fruit and cream or top with a dessert sauce.

3 large eggs, separated
1 tbs. flour
1 dash salt
1/2 tsp. vanilla extract

1/8 tsp. lemon extract
1/3 cup sugar
2 tbs. unsalted butter
confectioners' sugar for topping

Heat oven to 350.° In a medium bowl, beat egg yolks with flour, salt, vanilla and lemon extract. In a mixer bowl, beat egg whites until foamy and gradually beat in sugar. Whisk until stiff peaks form. Gently fold egg whites into egg yolks. Melt butter over very low heat in an 8-inch nonstick skillet with ovenproof handle. Pour in egg mixture and cook until barely browned on the bottom. Place on top shelf of oven and bake for 10 to 15 minutes until top is puffed and golden brown. Slide onto serving plate. Sprinkle with confectioners' sugar. Makes 2 servings.

STRAWBERRY JAM DESSERT OMELET

This is sure to be a hit with the kids. It's a quick and easy dessert to finish a meal or serve after a salad for lunch. If making it for adults, substitute some Triple Sec for the orange juice.

2 large eggs
2 tsp. milk or orange juice
2 tsp. sugar
1/8–1/4 tsp. vanilla extract
1 dash salt
2 tsp. unsalted butter
1 *Basic Dessert* or *Puffy Viennese Dessert Omelet,* pages 68 or 69
1 tbs. whipped cream cheese
1 tbs. strawberry jam
confectioners' sugar

Make *Basic Dessert* or *Puffy Viennese Dessert Omelets.* Fill with cream cheese and jam. Roll and dust with confectioners' sugar if desired.

BANANA RUM OMELETS

Here's a flaming dessert recipe.

2 large ripe bananas
3 tbs. unsalted butter
1/4 cup brown sugar
3 tbs. dark rum
2 *Basic Dessert Omelets,* page 68

Peel bananas. Slice in half lengthwise and cut into quarters. Melt butter and sugar in a skillet. Add banana quarters and sauté until well coated with butter and sugar, about 1 to 2 minutes. Do not overcook.

Prepare *Basic Dessert Omelets.* Divide banana filling and use 1/2 in each omelet before folding. Pour rum over omelets, flame and serve on warm plates. Makes enough filling for 2 omelets.

MANDARIN ORANGE OMELET

This is a refreshing dessert.

1 can (11 oz.) Mandarin orange segments
1 1/2 tsp. cornstarch
2 tbs. sugar
2 tbs. Triple Sec
1/2 cup sour cream
three *Basic Dessert Omelets,* page 68

Drain orange segments, reserving juice. Place juice in a small saucepan. Use 2 tbs. of the juice to dissolve cornstarch. Add dissolved cornstarch and sugar to saucepan. Bring to a boil. Simmer, stirring constantly, until sauce thickens. Add orange segments and heat through. Remove saucepan from heat and stir in Triple Sec. Prepare dessert omelets. Stir sour cream into orange filling. Fill omelets with orange mixture before folding. Makes approximately 1 3/4 cups filling, enough for 3 omelets.

PINEAPPLE DESSERT OMELET

This is a tropical dessert featuring pineapple and rum.

1 can (8 oz.) sliced unsweetened pineapple with juice
¼ cup brown sugar
1 tsp. cornstarch
2 tbs. dark rum
1 tbs. butter
4 *Basic Dessert Omelets,* page 68
fresh mint leaves for garnish

Drain pineapple juice into a small saucepan. Cut pineapple slices in half and set aside. Add brown sugar to pineapple juice and bring to a boil. Dissolve cornstarch in dark rum. Add cornstarch mixture and butter to pineapple juice. Cook over low heat, stirring, until sauce thickens. Remove from heat. Add pineapple slices.

Prepare and cook *Basic Dessert Omelets.* Before folding, fill with pineapple slices and a little of the sauce. Use remaining sauce for topping and garnish plates with mint leaves. Makes enough filling for 4 omelets.

CHERRY BRANDY SAUCE

Here is a good filling or sauce for dessert omelets. Try it with the Basic Dessert Omelet, *page 68.*

1 can (16 oz.) tart red pitted cherries with juice
1/2 cup sugar
1/8 tsp. cinnamon
1 tsp. lemon juice
1/8 tsp. almond extract
2 tbs. brandy
2 tsp. cornstarch dissolved in 2 tbs. cold water
2–3 *Basic Dessert Omelets*
confectioners' sugar for garnish, optional

Drain juice from cherries into a small saucepan. Add sugar, cinnamon, lemon juice, almond extract and brandy. Bring to a boil and cook until sugar dissolves. Dissolve cornstarch in cold water and add to cherry juice. Cook for 2 to 3 minutes, stirring, until sauce thickens. Stir in cherries. Use for a dessert omelet filling and topping. Sprinkle with confectioners' sugar if desired. Makes enough filling for 2 to 3 omelets.

APPLE OMELET

Apples, cream cheese and cinnamon make a nice sweet finish.

2 Golden Delicious or other
   cooking apples, peeled,
   cored and diced (about 3
   cups)
2 tbs. unsalted butter
2 tbs. water
3 tbs. sugar

$^{1}/_{2}$ tsp. cinnamon
$^{1}/_{8}$ tsp. nutmeg
3 *Basic Dessert Omelets,*
   page 68
3–4 tbs. whipped cream
   cheese
confectioners' sugar for garnish

   Melt butter over medium heat in a large skillet. Add apples and cook for 2 to 3 minutes to coat with butter. Add water and sugar, lower heat and cover. Cook for 5 to 6 minutes or until apples are soft. Stir occasionally. Remove lid and add cinnamon and nutmeg. Continue to cook until liquid evaporates. Reserve $^{1}/_{3}$ of the apple mixture for topping. Fill each omelet with cream cheese and apples. Spoon reserved apples over top of omelet and dust with confectioners' sugar if desired. Makes enough filling for 3 omelets.

INDEX

INDEX